What do I say now?

Answers for awkward questions and comments about adoption

By Carol Bick and M.C. Baker
Illustrations by Sophie Meyer

2B Publications
whatdoisaynow.co

Requests for permission to make copies of any part of this book should be mailed to the following address:

2B Publications

194 Davis Ave.

Shelburne, Vermont 05482

First Printing May 2015

Cover & Interior Design by Jocelyn Sargent

ISBN: 978-0-9904428-9-9

2B Publications

whatdoisaynow.co

For Ziva...You are my wish granted.
-M.C.B

For my two amazing daughters
whom I adore with all my heart
Lienne & Sophie
-CB

An invisible red thread connects those
who are destined to meet regardless of time, place, or circumstance.
The thread may stretch or tangle but will never break.
—Ancient Chinese Proverb

TABLE OF CONTENTS

INTRODUCTION: WHAT DO I SAY NOW?

If you are reading this book, chances are you are a parent who has adopted or is about to adopt, a child who entered her/his family through adoption, a friend or relative of a family brought together by adoption, or a mental health professional who is interested in the adoption world.

This book helps when people who usually mean well--but may know very little about the process of adoption--say the wrong thing!

For some reason, many people feel free to ask extremely personal questions when it comes to adoption. For example, "How much did he cost?" is one of the more common questions this book addresses. This example and many more situations are presented where having a ready-made answer may come in handy.

It's also about starting conversations with family and friends about adoption issues. If you are a parent or child who has been through the adoption process, you most likely have been asked many of the questions and/or been presented with some of the comments in this book and may have been at a loss how to respond.

Sometimes, the questions provide an opportunity to educate people about adoption. However, if you are tired, hungry, cranky or in a rush, you may not see educating others as a priority. There are times you might just want to give a quick answer and be on your way. This book also offers the "quick fix" response. However, not all the situations in this book are amenable to this kind of answer.

Hopefully, our suggestions will generate ideas on how to answer questions when you are thinking to yourself, "What do I say now?"

We have divided this book into three sections.

Part 1 focuses on questions and comments that children direct to other children. With parent and child reading together, discussing, problem solving, and role playing, you may better equip your children to handle whatever life may throw their way.

Part 2 deals with questions and comments that children direct to their parents. There are no right or wrong answers. However, being aware that these questions might be asked and having an idea how you might answer them, will help you feel prepared and increase your comfort level.

Part 3 delves into questions and comments that other adults direct to parents. These suggestions will give strategies that may aid in negotiating all those tricky questions that life's curious onlookers will throw your way. You may find some of the questions surprising, but these are situations where we can all share a chuckle and knowing shake of the head. Prior to adopting, we would never have believed that people could ask us such personal and intimate details. We only wish this book existed for our families!

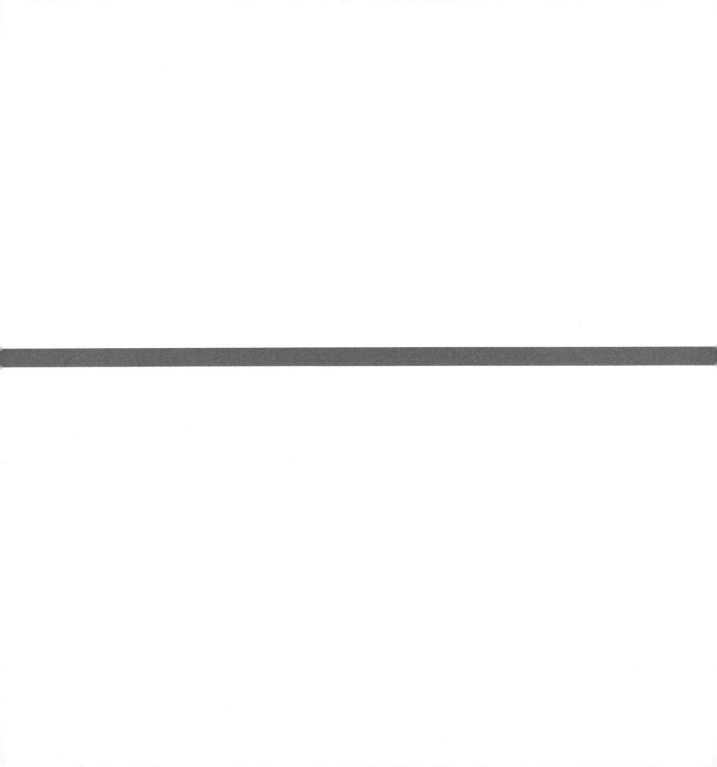

PART 1

QUESTIONS AND COMMENTS CHILDREN
DIRECT TO OTHER CHILDREN

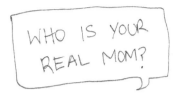

SCENARIO 1

Two children are playing Go Fish when Julie asks Rebecca: "Who is your real mom?"

Quick fix

"My mom is my real mom. I don't have a pretend one."

Raising awareness

"Do you mean my birth mom? Her name is Debra. The mom I live with is my real mom." If the other child goes on to say, "But you didn't come from your mom's belly," the next response could be, "You're right, I didn't come from her belly, but she's still my real mom." Do you have any queens? The other child says, "Go fish."

Take home message

Young children think concretely and in black and white. If you didn't come from your mother's body than she isn't your "real mom." The child feels that her parents are "real" but also knows that she has another set of parents and this can be confusing. It can be helpful to role-play these kinds of situations in order for your child to feel comfortable answering questions of this nature. One technique to keep in mind is to change the subject if the topic is too uncomfortable.

Carol's story

When my children were young, we would talk about what it meant to be a "real" parent. I would tell them that a real parent was someone who takes care of you and loves you no matter what. I often overheard my daughters mimic these words to other children who asked this exact question.

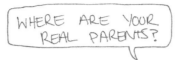

SCENARIO 2

Two children are talking while eating their lunch. Eli, who is adopted, says that his parents are away on vacation. The other child, who is aware that Eli is adopted, asks, "Do you know where your real parents are?"

Quick fix

"I just told you, they're on an adult vacation and I couldn't go because I'm not an adult."

Raising awareness

"If you're asking about my birth parents, I don't know."

Take home message

Children who know more about adoption are less likely to tease or make fun of children who enter a family through adoption. When children who are adopted educate other children on what proper terminology to use, they are expanding other childrens' knowledge of the adoption process as well as building their own self-confidence.

It is easier for children born in this country to access information about their biological parents and possibly meet them. In "open" adoptions, the child is able to contact the birth parents and/or have on-going relationships with them. In "closed" adoptions, the question of searching for the biological parents is not an easy one and can lead to both positive and challenging outcomes.

Charles Dickens once said, "To conceal anything from those to whom I am attached, is not in my nature. I can never close my lips where I have opened my heart." In most cases, the more open and honest families are about the child's adoption story and their biological parents, the better.

SCENARIO 3

Older brother David and younger sister Amelia are each eating a bowl of cereal at the breakfast table. They are getting ready for school and parents are rushing around.

Amelia says, "Phoebe said Luke is not my cousin.
David says, "Of course he is!"
Amelia says, "Yes, but not my REAL cousin."

Raising awareness

Ask, "Why do you think Phoebe said that?"

Listen to the child's answer. Most likely it will be because the cousin was adopted, that makes him somehow not her relative. This is where you need to look your child in the eye and say, "We are all a family. Families are brought together in many ways. Our family was brought together by adoption and we can't imagine life without Luke. What a gift!"

Take home message

Here's another time where the quick fix answer wouldn't be appropriate. When this situation comes up, it's because the young child does not know about adoption. The child may be repeating what they have heard. Take a deep breath and start the conversation.

Learning is a lifelong process. We are all growing and changing. As a parent or relative, it just feels bad to think that someone could doubt the intense love you feel for your child.

SCENARIO 4

Two children are sitting at their desks in a classroom. Asa, who is adopted, is talking about an adoption party he went to. Micah, who isn't adopted, says: "How come your mom and dad gave you up?"

Quick fix

"They weren't ready to be parents."

Raising awareness

"My birth parents chose adoption because they weren't able to take care of me. They made the decision that it would be better for me to be brought up by parents who were ready and able to take care of me and I'm really glad they did."

Take home message

How to answer this depends on the age and maturity level of the child. You might want to ask your child how he would want to answer this question. Role-playing may also help your child feel more comfortable if and when the situation arises.

The casual phrase of "giving up" implies a great deal about the child and birth parents. The connotations with this kind of language can lead to a sense of worthlessness for the child and irresponsibility on the part of the birth parent. These words can be hurtful and can lead to negative attitudes about adoption. Hopefully, by changing adoption language, attitudes about adoption will change. The old saying about "sticks and stones" is not true—words are powerful and can cause harm.

Please refer to the appendix at the end of this book for information on positive adoption language.

SCENARIO 5

Emma and her friends are at a school dance. A boy comes over to the group and starts to talk with Emma. He tells her that her shirt is pretty. Jodi, her jealous friend, makes a snide remark. "Her shirt isn't pretty. She has weird eyes, and she's adopted!"

Quick fix

"Why do you want to say hurtful things to me? I thought we were friends?"

Raising awareness

"My eyes are different from yours because I'm Chinese. They aren't weird, and I am adopted-so what?"

Take home message

Situations such as this one presents itself when the child matures into pre-adolescence. During this stage of development, most children want to "fit in" and not be singled out in any way. If the child doesn't already have friends and/or relatives that are adopted, this would be the time to make sure the child has other people in her life with whom she can identify.

For some children who are adopted, it can be challenging not to see other people who share similar physical characteristics. This may lead the child to feel she doesn't belong or fit in.

Role-playing situations like the one mentioned above can give your child an opportunity to try out possible responses. Brainstorming all the funny things you would like to say can also lighten the moment.

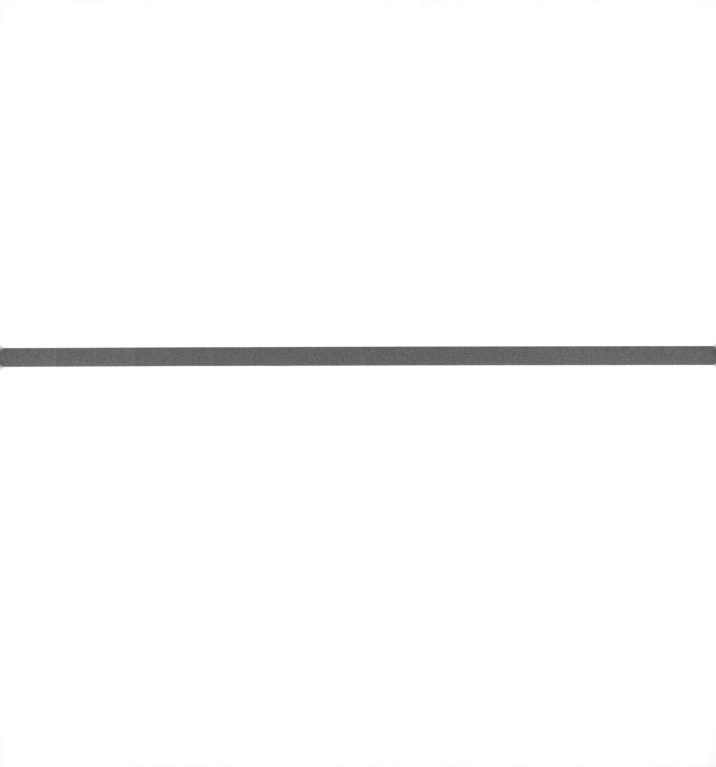

PART 2

QUESTIONS AND COMMENTS CHILDREN
DIRECT TO THEIR PARENTS

SCENARIO 6

Two dads are walking with their daughter, Maya, who was born in Guatemala. Maya asks, "Am I ever going to meet my birth parents?"

Raising awareness

"So you have been thinking about your birth parents? Do you want to meet them?"

Take home message

This is one of the situations that is not conducive to a quick fix answer. This kind of active listening strategy allows you to find out what the child is thinking and lets the child know you are really interested in what she has to say.

Associating with people from your child's culture helps in many ways. It sends a message that you value her and gives her a sense of identification with her own unique culture. It also goes a long way in helping the child not feel isolated as well as have a connection to the community.

There are adoption groups in many communities. Children who participate in these groups often get the chance not only to make friends with other kids who are adopted, but also connect with children who come from the same country. They realize that there are other kids like them and they aren't so different after all.

SCENARIO 7

A young child to her father: "How come your eyes are green and mine are brown and mom's eyes are blue?"

Quick fix

"That's the way we were made."

Raising awareness

"Your birth parents probably have brown eyes."

M.C.'s story

Sometimes a younger child needs only quick answers. My daughter Ziva asked me this question when she was three, while we were reading bedtime stories. Inside my head I thought, "Oh no! Here come all the questions!" Instinctively, I gave her the reply, "I bet your birth mom had brown eyes." As I was thinking about what I should say next and how to phrase it, Ziva flipped back onto her back and grabbed the book. She was done taking about our eye color and had moved on.

This moment taught me a valuable lesson. A detailed and complicated explanation may not be what is needed at a particular time. However, talking about adoption and bringing up the terms "birth parents" or "biological parents" at a very young age allows the child to be familiar with this language. The child's understanding of what adoption means will deepen and change over time. By using this language in everyday conversations, your child will grow up to be comfortable with the terminology and the process of adoption.

In addition, it's a good idea to include, among the children's books in your home, books with characters who are adopted as well as different family configurations such as same sex parents, single parent families, foster families, blended families, and grandparents as the primary caregivers.

SCENARIO 8

Dylan is holding hands with his parent. Dylan asks: "Do you think my birth parents loved me?"

Quick fix

"I really don't know, but we sure love you."

Raising awareness

"What your birth parents did by placing you for adoption was probably the hardest thing they ever did. They cared for you enough to realize they weren't in a position to take care of you. They worked with an adoption agency (or lawyer) to find us and we're so very lucky they did!"

Take home message

Every situation involving adoption is unique and the answers to these kinds of questions need to be individualized. While intellectually, the child understands that he did nothing wrong and that it was the birth parent's choice to decide on adoption, the visceral feeling may be that he isn't worthy, because if he was "good enough," the birth parent would have kept him.

Sometimes the choice for a child to be placed for adoption is not voluntary. In cases where abuse and/or neglect is the issue and the child is aware of it, the answer may contain something like, "I don't know why your mom did what she did and I can't answer the question about how she felt. I can tell you that I am blessed to have you in my life and love you very much."

SCENARIO 9

A child is cuddling with his mom and he says, "I wish I came from your body."

Raising awareness

"I've thought about that too but then realized you wouldn't be who you are and I wouldn't want to change one thing about you!"

Take home message

There are challenges with adopting and we need to be honest with ourselves and our children when these kinds of issues arise. Many parents who adopt connect with others who create their families through adoption. Discussing and sharing stories can be helpful and healing.

Carol's story

Both of my children have made this comment and I responded with the words above. I have also talked to them about our being meant to be with each other, which I truly believe.

My husband and I created adoption books when the children were young. It started from when we first thought about adoption up until we met our children. They were favorite books in our house and read over and over again. Having an adoption book helps children better understand what adoption is and how much they are wanted and treasured.

SCENARIO 10

A dad is talking to his daughter, Ruby. She is about to meet Ari, who is being adopted from Russia. Ruby asks her dad, "Do we get to send Ari back if we don't like him?"

Quick fix

"No honey, Ari is your brother. He's here to stay!"

Raising awareness

"Once someone is part of our family, they are family forever. There may be times that you'll get annoyed with Ari, but family is family and we work out our differences."

Take home message

This question is often asked, whether the new child joins the family by adoption or birth. It can be tricky if the family is made up of children who are adopted and biological. Keeping your sense of humor is helpful. However, if the parents truly believe that one way to bring children into the family is no better than the other, the children will believe this as well.

It's a good idea to talk about the many different ways families are created. Children may be afraid of change, yet we ask them to change so much in their formative years, we can sometimes forget it is difficult to really internalize changes. Being flexible thinkers with each new situation will help. Even when things are not working as well as you hoped, the fact that you are working at the relationship means that it will work--maybe just not on the timeline you had wanted!

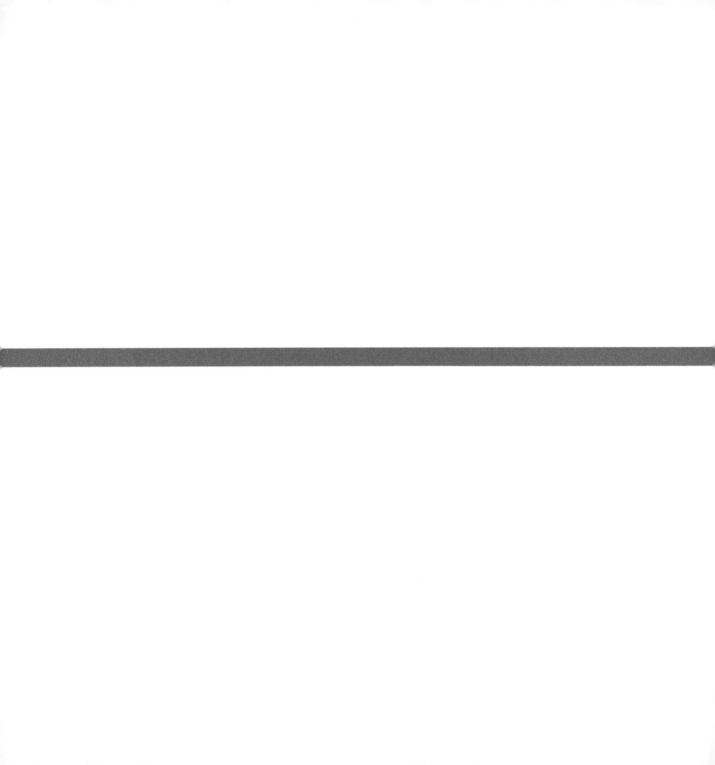

PART 3

QUESTIONS AND COMMENTS ADULTS
DIRECT TO PARENTS WHO ADOPT

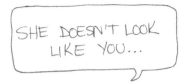

SCENARIO 11

A mother and her toddler daughter, who is from South Korea, are at the library, participating in a read-aloud group. Another mother, who is sitting with her son says, "She doesn't look like you."

Quick fix

"No she doesn't, but I wish I looked liked her—Isn't she adorable?"

Raising awareness

"Charlotte is adopted from South Korea. She may not look like me but she is surely my daughter."

Take home message

People are naturally curious and will ask questions or make comments about your family. This is only exacerbated if you do not look like your child.

Don't be afraid to say that you became a family through adoption or that your child was born in South Korea. In the end, your child gains confidence and skills by hearing you state the facts in a positive tone. Try to remind yourself that people are curious. Just meet their questions as honestly as you can without being sarcastic or sharing too much of your personal family information. Of course, there is a difference when people ask because of a real interest or connection and when they are asking just to be nosy.

One strategy that is often talked about in the adoption world is to give two similarities for every difference. When a situation comes up where a difference is noticed, a parent might say something like, "She might not look like us but she's a math whiz like me and is a great cook just like her dad." Children love to hear how they are like their parents as well as how they are unique unto themselves.

M.C.'s story

My family has faced many questions over the years. The grocery store is ripe for these situations. More often there are smiles and kind glances in our direction. Sometimes I ask Ziva, "Why do you think that lady is staring at us?" I will often recreate a situation and say. "Ziva, let's think of other ways we could have answered that person." I love to role-play because it allows me to process a particular situation, get a feel for how my daughter felt (or is feeling), and turn things into a learning opportunity.

SCENARIO 12

A visiting neighbor asks the parent who just adopted: "How much did Ona cost?" Believe it or not, this is a common question that many people who adopt are asked.

Raising awareness

"We used the "X" adoption agency. You could give them a call if you're interested in adopting," or "We did have to pay the adoption agency (or lawyer) for helping bring Ona into our lives. It's not much different from paying for services at a hospital when giving birth."

Take home message

It can be very tempting to answer in a "snarky" way. However, it doesn't help in the long run and we usually feel bad if we do reply this way. We also need to be positive role models for our children as well as helping other people understand more about the adoption process.

Talking about money and adoption can be confusing to children. It's important for children to understand that we don't "buy" people. It's also essential that adults don't talk about this topic to other adults when young children are present. This is a difficult concept to comprehend and little ones may misinterpret the conversation.

Carol's story

A friend of mine got so tired of being asked this question that she made up cards with her information on them and gave them to people who asked this intrusive question. She would say something like, "I'm busy right now, but if you are really interested in adoption, please give me a call."

SCENARIO 13

Two women have just adopted a child from China. One of the moms is talking to her aunt on the phone. The aunt asks: "Are you going to tell people Eva is adopted?"

Quick fix

"Of course I am."

Raising awareness

"What would be the value in not telling other people that Eva's adopted?

Take home message

The second option may start a conversation on adoption issues and raise awareness about adoption. Even today, some people still think adoption is not as good as giving birth. It is almost as if they believe parents should pretend the children they adopt are their biological offspring.

This question doesn't come up as much with inter-racial and some inter-country adoptions because the physical differences are obvious except in cases like this situation where the aunt is clueless.

SCENARIO 14

A father is holding his daughters' hands. The girls look very different: one has dark skin and the other is light. Another man asks, "Are they sisters?"

Quick fix

"Yes, they are."

Raising awareness

"Yes they are. Sienna was born in Haiti and became part of our family by adoption, and Indira is our biological child. They are not related by blood, but they are definitely sisters."

Take home message

Some people have no problem asking personal questions. People seem to need to "connect the dots" when they are confused about family configurations. The more casual and matter-of-fact the answer, the more comfortable the listener will feel about the adoption process.

Adoption statistics show a steady decline in international adoption. There were about 19,000 international adoptions in 2000 and about 8,000 in 2012. The top five adopting countries are: China, Ethiopia, Russia, South Korea and Ukraine. For more information on international adoptions, you could refer to the Intercountry Adoption Bureau of Consular Affairs at the US Department of State.

SCENARIO 15

A dad and his son are at the post office. The person behind the counter asks, "Where does your child come from?"

Quick fix

"We live in Vermont."

Raising Awareness

"Ezra was born in Ethiopia."

Take home message

This question is usually asked when the child's facial features and/or skin color look different from his parents'. Being open about adoption and sharing information goes a long way toward diminishing myths that have been with us for ages. However, you may not always be in the right mood to start this conversation. Parents, give yourself permission to sometimes take the quick fix option. We all need a break once in a while!

M.C.'s story

This scenario actually happened to my daughter and me. Before I could say anything, Ziva shouted out that she was from "Westford." When the gentleman looked confused, Ziva said again, "Westford, Vermont." I chuckled at this point and prompted Ziva that I thought the man was curious about where she was born. That is when she said, "Oh. China." Ziva is our daughter, period. Being adopted is only one part of what makes us a family.

SCENARIO 16

Two couples are out for dinner, talking about their children. One person says to the couple that just adopted, "Leo is so lucky to have you."

Quick fix

"We're the lucky ones."

Raising awareness

"I can see how you might think that. However, we feel incredibly fortunate and believe we are all lucky to have each other."

Take home message

There used to be a show called "Kids Say The Darndest Things." Well, so do adults! People are usually well meaning, but can say things that hurt.

People adopt because they want to be parents, not out of charity. Waiting up to five years is not unheard of in the adoption world. The usual response to the phone call alerting you that your child is here, is to yell, scream, jump up and down, cry, and feel like you are the luckiest person alive. You are!

SCENARIO 17

A mom and her toddler daughter are in line at the supermarket checkout counter. The older woman behind her is playing "peek-a-boo" with the toddler. The woman says, "She's adorable! I bet she looks just like her father."

Quick fix

"You are right, she is adorable!"

Raising awareness

"Actually, Tess is adopted, and I didn't get to meet her biological parents. However, she does have my partner's outgoing personality, and her artistic talent comes from me."

Take home message

While the children we adopt may not look like us, chances are they will take on some of our interests and talents. The age-old question—environment or heredity—well, we do know that environment plays a big part of who we are.

People seem to need to actually see similarities between child and parent. When the child and parent don't resemble each other, people usually assume the child looks like the other parent. Children who are adopted often like to have similarities pointed out between them and their parents. The raising awareness option allows the child to hear that she is in some way similar to a parent as well as stating the fact that she is adopted.

Being adopted is only one characteristic of the child. It does not define her. When parents hesitate to let people know that their child is adopted, the child senses there is something wrong with being adopted. The child will feel the parents' comfort or discomfort in the way the parent answers these questions. Some people believe that it should be left up to the child whether other people know she is adopted. As parents who have adopted, we feel strongly that adoption is not something that needs to be hidden. People tend to hide things they are ashamed about and adoption should not be categorized as shameful.

Depending on the age of your child, it might be a good idea to undertake this conversation with your child later. Asking the child, "Do you have any thoughts about what that woman said in the supermarket?" may be a good starting point. As children get older, it's a good idea to let them take the lead in such situations.

SCENARIO 18

Uncle Bob, who is planning on adopting, is talking to his niece. His niece asks, "Why would you want to bring up someone else's child?"

Quick fix

"Caleb will be my child."

Raising awareness

"I believe that the people we love become our family. I know I will adore Caleb and while he didn't come from me biologically, he definitely will come from my heart. I'm sure you'll fall in love the minute you meet your new cousin."

Take home message

We have no control over what other people think, but we do have control over how we respond to them. Answering in an honest, respectful manner without being defensive is the best strategy. If the person is a relative or close friend and will be spending time with the child, she will most likely fall in love with your child too, and feel this child is her "own" nephew, grandchild or cousin.

SCENARIO 19

A single dad is driving his babysitter home. The babysitter asks, "Why did you want to adopt?"

Quick fix

"I wanted to have a family."

Raising awareness

"I wanted to be a parent but was not interested in being married. I believe adoption is a great way to create a family."

Take home message

Children and teens often ask these kinds of questions because they are genuinely curious. You may or may not want to go into specifics about why you chose to adopt. Most, if not all people who adopt, just want to be parents. Having children is an essential part of many people's lives.

For many, infertility is the main reason. Some people may choose to adopt because of other medical or genetic reasons. Other people choose adoption as the preferred way to enlarge their family. Single people as well as people who are married to someone of the same gender often choose adoption as a way to create their family.

Whatever the reason, this is one of the easier questions to answer: "I wanted to be a parent."

SCENARIO 20

A man, who is Caucasian, and his daughter, Fay, who is a child of color, are waiting in line to get ice cream. They are happily discussing what flavor to order. Fay shouts out, "Vanilla with rainbow sprinkles!" The man in front of them smiles back at both the dad and at Fay and asks, "Is your wife black?"

Quick fix

"No, my husband happens to be Caucasian as well."

Take home message

This often happens when you don't look like your child. While trying to be patient is important, it doesn't always work. The bottom line is your child is the one who matters.

M.C.'s story

My daughter is Asian. When we were taking a family vacation in China, we were stopped and stared at very often. It was something we tried to get used to. One evening after an exhausting day of traffic, tourist spots, and confusion, we were heading back to our hotel room. We were almost there when a group of tourists maneuvered themselves into the elevator with us. We noticed "the look" immediately, and afterwards, a polite smile. When they finally left the elevator, my husband, daughter and I pealed with laughter. It was perfect. We didn't even have to say anything—sharing laughter as a family was the best medicine.

Carol's story

I walked into a dry cleaning establishment with Sophie when she was an infant. The clerk behind the counter asked, "Why would a nice Jewish girl like you marry a black man?"

This is one of those times I wish I had been prepared with a good comeback. While I don't remember what I said, I do remember never stepping foot in that shop again.

SCENARIO 21

Two women are pushing baby carriages. One woman is a birth mom and the other mom adopted her baby. The birth mother says, "I never think of Corina as adopted. She seems just like your own daughter."

Quick fix

"Corina is my own daughter."

Raising awareness

"I know you didn't mean this statement to be hurtful, but when you said you don't think of Corina as adopted, you were implying that adoption is in some way negative. Just like her beautiful green eyes and wonderful personality, adoption is part of who Corina is and I don't want to disregard any part of her."

Carol's story

Besides mentioning adoption in this kind of scenario, people often talk about race and/ or ethnicity. The race situation happened to me with a neighbor. Lienne (who was about five at the time) and I were walking in our neighborhood. We stopped to talk to a woman who we knew slightly. The woman smiled and said, "I never think of Lienne as black."

I believe I responded with something like, "Lienne is bi-racial and I love her skin color."

It's important to let people know that you want them to think of your child for who she is including her race, ethnicity, and adoption status. These are important aspects of your child and they should all be appreciated.

APPENDIX: SPEAKING OF ADOPTION IN POSITIVE TERMS

People often talk about adoption in negative terms simply because those are the terms they've always heard. It can help to have a more positive word or phrase to offer in place of the familiar, prejudicial language. Also, rephrasing a situation can get people to think about it in an entirely new light.

Negative	Positive
Giving away your child	Making an adoption plan for your child or relinquishing your child
Putting your child up for adoption	Finding a family to parent your child
Giving up your child	Placing the child in an adoptive home
Real or natural mother	Birth mother or biological mother
Real or natural father	Father of the baby or biological father
Real family	First family
Adoptive family	Forever family
Real child or natural child	Child by birth or biological child
Illegitimate child	Child of unmarried parents
Reunion	Meeting between birth parents and child who was adopted

ACKNOWLEDGMENTS

Special thanks to Tim Brookes, our invaluable editor, Sandra Barone, Sarah Schoolcraft, Ann Clark, the students at Champlain College in the Publishing in the 21st Century class, Jocelyn Sargent, Wide Horizon For Children, the students and families who were brought together through adoption at Williston Central School, and of course our amazing family and friends that have been with us through it all.

ABOUT THE AUTHORS AND ILLUSTRATOR

M.C. Baker

MC received her Bachelor and Master of Architecture degree from Savannah College of Art and Design. She lives in Westford, Vermont with her husband, Greg, her daughter, Ziva. They have a passion for traveling and love just being together as a family.

Carol Bick

Carol received her BA in Social Work from Trinity College in Vermont and her MS in counseling from the University of Vermont. Carol lives in Shelburne, Vermont with her husband, Bob and beloved dogs. Carol is the parent of two daughters who were adopted in infancy. Lienne entered their family when she was ten days old and Sophie at five days. Both girls are now adults with families of their own.

Sophie Meyer

Sophie received her Bachelor of Music from Berklee College of Music, where she studied song writing, and her MA in Higher Education Administration from California State University, Northridge. Sophie lives in Shelburne, Vermont with her husband and lovable dog, TJ. Sophie joined her family—parents, Bob and Carol, and sister, Lienne—by way of adoption at five days old.

CPSIA information can be obtained
at www.ICGtesting.com
Printed in the USA
BVHW02s2009200418
513912BV00019B/215/P